Business & Ethics

Young Adult Library of Small Business and Finance

Building a Business in the Virtual World

Business & Ethics

Business & the Government: Law and Taxes

Business Funding & Finances

Keeping Your Business Organized:
Time Management & Workflow

Managing Employees

Marketing Your Business

Starting a Business: Creating a Plan

Understanding Business Math & Budgets

What Does It Mean to Be an Entrepreneur?

Young Adult Library of Small Business and Finance

Business & Ethics

James Fischer

Mason Crest

Mason Crest
450 Parkway Drive, Suite D
Broomall, PA 19008
www.masoncrest.com

Printed in the United States of America.

First printing
9 8 7 6 5 4 3 2 1

Series ISBN: 978-1-4222-2912-5
Hardcover ISBN: 978-1-4222-2914-9
Paperback ISBN: 978-1-4222-2981-1
ebook ISBN: 978-1-4222-8904-4

The Library of Congress has cataloged the
hardcopy format(s) as follows:

Library of Congress Cataloging-in-Publication Data

Fischer, James, 1988-
  Business & ethics / James Fischer.
     pages cm. – (Young adult library of small business and finance)
  Audience: Grade 7 to 8.
  ISBN 978-1-4222-2914-9 (hardcover) – ISBN 978-1-4222-2912-5 (series) –
ISBN 978-1-4222-8904-4 (ebook) – ISBN 978-1-4222-2981-1 (paperback)
  1. Business ethics–Juvenile literature. I. Title.
  HF5387.F5647 2014
  174'.4–dc23
                                        2013015648

Produced by Vestal Creative Services.
www.vestalcreative.com

CONTENTS

INTRODUCTION

Brigitte Madrian, PhD

Small businesses serve a dual role in our economy. They are the bedrock of community life in the United States, providing goods and services that we rely on day in and day out. Restaurants, dry cleaners, car repair shops, plumbers, painters, landscapers, hair salons, dance studios, and veterinary clinics are only a few of the many different types of local small business that are part of our daily lives. Small businesses are also important contributors to the engines of economic growth and innovation. Many of the successful companies that we admire today started as small businesses run out of bedrooms and garages, including Microsoft, Apple, Dell, and Facebook, to name only a few. Moreover, the founders of these companies were all very young when they started their firms. Great business ideas can come from people of any age. If you have a great idea, perhaps you would like to start your own small business. If so, you may be wondering: What does it take to start a business? And how can I make my business succeed?

A successful small business rests first and foremost on a great idea—a product or service that other people or businesses want and are willing to pay for. But a good idea is not enough. Successful businesses start with a plan. A business plan defines what the business will do, who its customers will be, where the firm will be located, how the firm will market the company's product, who the firm will hire, how the business will be financed, and what, if any, are the firm's plans for future growth. If a firm needs a loan from a bank in order to start up, the bank will mostly likely want to see a written business plan. Writing a business plan helps an entrepreneur think

through all the possible road blocks that could keep a business from succeeding and can help convince a bank to make a loan to the firm.

Once a firm has the funding in place to open shop, the next challenge is to connect with the firm's potential customers. How will potential customers know that the company exists? And how will the firm convince these customers to purchase the company's product? In addition to finding customers, most successful businesses, even small ones, must also find employees. What types of employees should a firm hire? And how much should they be paid? How do you motivate employees to do their jobs well? And what do you do if employees don't get along? Managing employees is an important skill in running almost any successful small business.

Finally, firms must also understand the rules and regulations that govern how they operate their business. Some rules, like paying taxes, apply to all businesses. Other rules apply to only certain types of firms. Does the firm need a license to operate? Are there restrictions on where the firm can locate or when it can be open? What other regulations must the firm comply with?

Starting up a small business is a lot of work. But despite the hard work, most small business owners find their jobs

Business & Ethics

rewarding. While many small business owners are happy to have their business stay small, some go on to grow their firms into more than they ever imagined, big companies that service customers throughout the world.

What will your small business do?

Brigitte Madrian, PhD
Aetna Professor of Public Policy and Corporate Management
Harvard Kennedy School

 **Introduction**

ONE

What Are Ethics? And Why Are They Important?

From the time we're very young, we're taught what is right and what is wrong. We know it's wrong to cheat on a test or hurt someone out of anger. We know it's right to treat people fairly and be respectful.

Combined together, all the things that are right and wrong make up ethics. Ethics are standards of behavior we consider to be right and wrong. So cheating and hurting people are unethical. Treating people fairly and respectfully is ethical. Ethics can get a lot more complicated than that, but thinking about what is right and wrong will take you a long way toward understanding what ethics are.

Cheating on a test is an example of unethical behavior.

Business & Ethics

What Are Ethics (and What Aren't They)?

The Markkula Center for Applied Ethics tells a story about defining ethics. A few years ago, a **sociologist** named Raymond Baumhart asked a bunch of business people what they thought ethics meant. They told him a lot of different things. The answers didn't contain the whole truth, but they might help you understand this idea:

"Ethics has to do with what my feelings tell me is right or wrong."
Sometimes we feel like something is right or wrong in our hearts, although our feelings aren't always correct. You could feel like doing something wrong, like stealing a cookie from your little brother. Or you could feel like you don't want to do something right because it's too hard.

"Ethics has to do with my religious beliefs."
Religion does have a lot to do with ethics, and religions teach us to act ethically. A religion might encourage you to give to the poor, treat people with **compassion**, and always do what is right. But non-religious people can behave ethically too. We don't need religion to tell us what is ethical.

"Being ethical is doing what the law requires."
The law sometimes follows ethical ways of behaving. For example, it is illegal to harm other people. However, the law isn't

Ethical personal qualities are qualities that a society values.

always ethical, and is sometimes very unethical. Just think of slavery, which was completely legal for many years.

"Ethics consists of the standards of behavior our society accepts."

Society is made up of all the people who live in one area and share some things in common. Not everyone in a society thinks

Business & Ethics

exactly the same way. Our society accepts that it is not okay to kill someone, which is unethical, but it's divided about whether we should save human lives by using animals in experiments. We're not sure if animal testing is ethical or not.

None of these answers are quite right, but they all sort of get at what ethics is.

Remember, ethics are standards of behavior we consider to be right and wrong. The Markkula Center says ethics are made up of several things. Hurting, killing, and stealing from someone, for instance, are ethically wrong. Ethics also involves personal **qualities** like honesty, fairness, and compassion. An ethical person is honest, fair, and compassionate, among other good things. Finally, ethics has to do with rights, or things we believe all human beings should have. Rights include the right to life, the right to clean water and enough food, and the right to freedom of belief. Basically, ethics are the **values** that lead to people having good lives.

Some Ethical Examples

If you ever find yourself in a situation that has to do with ethics, you might have some trouble figuring out what to do. Just because you're dealing with ethics doesn't mean it's easy to figure out what is right and what is wrong. Here are a few ethical **dilemmas** you might face. Think about what you would do if you were in these situations—there isn't always an easy answer. You can find all of these dilemmas and more on the Scholastic News Sticky Situation website.

1. Khaleel is on a debate team. His friend Tania is on an opposing team. The two teams will soon face off. Tania sits next to Khaleel in class, and he realizes that he can see her debate notes. Khaleel knows that cheating is wrong, but the information in her notes could help his team win. What should Khaleel do?

   In some ethical dilemmas, you have to weigh what is right with what will happen if you act ethically. Khaleel knows it's wrong to cheat, and he knows he could get in trouble. But he also really wants to win the debate. Is doing what's right worth the risk?

2. Julisa's mom surprises her with a sweater that she knit herself. It took Julisa's mom weeks to make it. Julisa appreciates her mom's effort, but she thinks the sweater is ugly. Julisa doesn't want to wear the sweater, but she also doesn't want to hurt her mom's feelings. What should Julisa do?

   Sometimes ethics has to do with other people's feelings. When you act selfishly, you are often acting unethically. Julisa has to think about how much she could hurt her mom's feelings and figure out if she should wear the sweater or not.

3. Patricia is on the playground when she sees a group of older boys threatening Jonathan, a new boy at school. One of the boys tells Patricia to watch as he trips Jonathan. Other kids on the playground laugh and point as Jonathan falls to the ground. Patricia feels bad for Jonathan, but she doesn't want the older boys to bother her. What should Patricia do?

   Ethical dilemmas get hard when you have to think about your own safety. Patricia thinks helping Jonathan is the

Business & Ethics

right thing to do, but she also doesn't want to get hurt or teased.

4. Jordy and Arjun were playing a video game at Jordy's house. Arjun accidentally knocked over a glass of juice onto Jordy's computer. Jordy needs to get his computer repaired and thinks Arjun should pay for that. Arjun disagrees. He thinks it's Jordy's fault for keeping his drink too close to his computer. What should Arjun do?

Jordy and Arjun are having trouble figuring out what is right. Each one doesn't want to pay to get the computer fixed, which is getting in the way of figuring out an ethical solution.

Types of Ethics

APPLIED ETHICS

We can also talk about different kinds of ethics. The kind of ethics we care about in our everyday lives are called applied ethics. Applied ethics are how we think about and use ethics in our daily lives. Applied ethics are divided into different types.

Bioethics is the study of what is right and wrong when it comes to biological sciences. New scientific knowledge and technology has given people a lot of power over what happens with living things. Should we use that power? Bioethics asks and tries to answer questions about human **cloning**, changing our **genes**, and using animals for experiments.

Political ethics have to do with the government and the choices and actions politicians take. A political candidate who

BUSINESS ETHICS IN THE PAST

Back in the late 1800s and early 1900s, lots of businesses weren't making very ethical decisions. The game Monopoly is based on what was going on back then—big businesses gobbling up as much as they could buy. The owners of some businesses got very, very rich, like Andrew Carnegie and John D. Rockefeller. Meanwhile, their companies didn't treat their workers very well. And the big businesses put other, smaller companies out of business in order to grow as large as they could. On the other hand, the business owners who became very wealthy often donated millions of dollars to charities, schools, hospitals, museums, and more, and did a lot of good. Back then (and today), people practiced a lot of both good and bad business ethics.

steals money from his campaign is not being politically ethical. Political ethics also asks questions about whether government **policies** are ethically right or not.

Geoethics is a third kind of ethics. Geoethics focuses on how we treat the Earth and the environment. People who think about geoethics study whether or how we should deal with climate change, whether we should use up the world's **resources**, and if we should save forests and oceans.

Business & Ethics

Business Ethics

Another type of ethics is called business ethnics. Questions about what is right or wrong show up in business all the time. Ethical businesspeople try to do what is right.

In the business world, you have to make many decisions. What should you do with the money you make? How should you treat employees? Will you report the money you make to the government? Should you lie about your product to make more money? All these questions have to do with business rights and wrongs.

Being a good businessperson means having good business ethics. You might not always know what is right and wrong, but you try to follow good ethics. If you're unsure about what to do with your business, you can ask someone for help.

Ethics has always been important in business. Business owners and employees have always had to decide what was right and wrong, and how to run an ethical company. Plenty of other businesspeople have also had to deal with ethics and can help you out.

Business Ethics and Other People

Part of why ethics matters is because your decisions affect other people. If you decide to cheat on a test at school, you could get in trouble, but you could also get the other person in trouble. If you ended up with a high grade, while people who didn't cheat got lower grades, it wouldn't be fair. If you stole some clothes from the mall, you would be taking away the store's opportunity to sell the clothes and make money from them. Unethical behaviors hurt other people, or make their lives harder.

Most of the business decisions you make affect other people. If you own a babysitting business, for example, you deal with people all the time. Parents hire you. You take care of kids. Your actions affect those people.

You have plenty of chances to make unethical decisions if you run a babysitting business. You could decide to take the kids you're babysitting out of the house without telling their parents. Maybe it would turn out all right, but the kids could get hurt. Or you could steal money or jewelry from the house you're babysitting in.

Both of those things are unethical. You probably already know you shouldn't do them, and if you took the kids out of their house or stole, you would probably feel bad. You don't want to make yourself feel bad, so that's one good reason to avoid unethical actions.

Another way to think about it is to consider the other people involved. You're putting the kids in danger by taking them out of their house without their parents' permission. Or you're taking money away from people who worked hard, and who won't be able to pay for something now because they have less money.

However, when you make ethical choices, you help people out. If you promise the parents you'll keep the kids around the house and get them to bed at eight, you're helping them out. You're also keeping the kids safe and rested. Or if you happen to find a twenty-dollar bill under the couch, you could give it back to the parents. They'll thank you for it, and realize you're an honest person!

Business & Ethics

SOME UNETHICAL BUSINESS PROBLEMS

Businesses and the people in charge of business aren't always ethical. Here are some examples of ways businesses have been unethical. Take a lesson from them and avoid these decisions as your business grows.

- *Bribing* politicians to eventually get extra money for a company. Businesspeople have also given politicians money to change the law to benefit the company.
- Refusing to hire people based on their gender, *ethnicity*, religion, or anything else.
- Dumping poisonous waste from factories into the ground or water, where it could hurt the environment and the people who live nearby.
- Not paying workers enough, or forcing them to work in unsafe or unhealthy conditions.
- Advertising that a product does something that it doesn't do.

Why Business Ethics Matters to You

Ethics might seem like a complicated idea, but we all have to make ethical decisions all the time. Most of the time, it's easy, because we know what's wrong or right. You know you shouldn't steal or shove another person to the ground.

However, business ethics aren't always as clear. As a young person, you're just starting out in the business world. You'll need more experience to know what the most ethical business decision is for each situation you encounter. But you should always try to make business decisions that affect other people in a good way.

HOW TO MAKE ETHICAL DECISIONS

The Arizona Character Education Foundation lists four ways to tell if you're making an ethical decision or not:

1. Use the Golden Rule—treat others the way you want to be treated.
2. How would your actions look on the front page of a newspaper, or as the headline of a news program?
3. What if your family was watching? Would you want them to know what you're doing?
4. Apply the principle of universality: consider whether your actions would be good if everyone in the world did them.

Think over one or all of these guidelines the next time you have to make a tough ethical decision.

If you want to start a business, or already run one, ethics are especially important. The rest of these chapters will help you figure out just how to make the most ethical decisions when it comes to business. But you'll need to use your own head—do what seems right, and ask advice when you need it!

TWO

Ethics and Goal-Setting

Goals are like the destinations of journeys. We want to do work now so we can arrive at our goals later. In business, people have a lot of goals, like making a good product, making money, and helping other people.

Goals aren't the only things that matter, though. How people reach goals also matters. Along the way, people need to figure out how to reach their goals ethically, by doing what's right.

Business Goals

Part of running a business is setting goals. Ask yourself what you want out of your business. Some young ***entrepreneurs*** want to make a lot of money. Some want to help other people. Some want to learn a lot.

Making money shouldn't be your primary goal. If making money becomes more important than running an ethical business, you should take another look at your goals.

Business & Ethics

START YOUR BUSINESS ONLINE

Maybe you have a great idea for a business, but you haven't started it quite yet. Check out bizinate.com to get you going. Bizinate is a company committed to helping other people start companies! The site lets you start your own webpage, advertise, and even sell stuff right there online—it's all in one place. You'll have to sign up and pay a one-time fee, but then you're all set. The Internet has all sorts of resources to help you start your own business. Search around for other websites geared toward helping young people start their own businesses.

Goals can be a little dangerous, though. If you make your goals more important than anything else, you might be tempted to do some unethical things to achieve them. Before you make any decisions, you should stop and ask yourself if they are ethical decisions.

Let's go back to the babysitting example. Your goal is to make money to save up for college. You also like working with kids, and you want some more experience with them. You have good goals, so now you have to make some choices about how to achieve them.

First, you may have to ask people for some money to set up your business. You'll need money to print flyers to advertise your

babysitting business. You need a little money to buy and set up a website. You also need some money for a babysitting course at the Red Cross. Altogether, you only need about $50. You think your parents will give you the money, because they're proud you're starting your own business.

You could, however, decide to tell them you really need more than $50. If you ask for more money, you can use the extra money to go to the movies and eat out with friends. Asking for extra money, though, would be dishonest and unethical.

You may also want to exaggerate how good your business is. You need to get customers to hire you to babysit their kids. You could lie and say you've babysat many times, to make people

A BIG MISTAKE

Barry Minkow was a teenage business genius. By the time he was sixteen, Barry had started a carpet-cleaning business. He quickly became a millionaire, and he started buying things like cars and an expensive house. He had big plans for his business, but unfortunately a lot of those plans were unethical and illegal. He charged customers too much money for the work he did. In the end, he **swindled** $100 million from customers and investors. The government found out, and he was sent to prison for several years. Barry had chosen to do some unethical things in the quest to make lots of money and run a successful business.

Business & Ethics

think you're more experienced than you really are. You could also choose not to take the babysitting course, but then say you did. Both of those decisions would also be dishonest. They could even put the kids you'll be babysitting in danger because you don't know what you're doing. The ethical thing to do would be to take the course, and tell customers exactly how much experience you've had. Then they can decide whether to hire you. Chances are, someone will give you a shot at babysitting, and they'll see how great at it you are because you've taken the time to learn. Then you can slowly build your customers, honestly and ethically.

Corporate Social Responsibility

Goals themselves can also be ethical or unethical. If your business goal is to make your friend look bad, you're being unethical. On the other hand, if your business goal is to provide a service like babysitting for busy parents who really need help, you're being ethical. Something called "*corporate* social responsibility" has a lot to do with the goals businesses set. Corporate social responsibility is a long way of saying that some businesses choose to make the world a better place. They are choosing to be responsible to the world. A business whose goal is corporate social responsibility is making an ethical choice.

Businesses can do a few things to make the world a better place. They can donate money to good causes. A company that makes houses might donate money to charities that provide housing for *low-income* families, for example.

Businesses can also make sure the materials they use to make their products come from ethical sources. A responsible business will make sure the people who make their products are paid well. It will make sure the materials it uses are not polluting or destroying the environment.

What does that mean for you and your company? Corporate social responsibility means that you can make the world a better place with your business, no matter how big or small your business is. Whatever you do with your business will affect other people—so why not affect other people in a good way?

Let's say you have a good business idea: you want to make and sell handmade greeting cards. You're really good at art, and one of your goals is to make some money. You also like to help people, so your other goal is to help people with your business.

You start looking around at materials to make your cards. You go to the craft store and look through the paper they have. You know paper comes from trees, and you want to make sure the paper you use isn't destroying forests. You do some research online about the brands of paper you found at the craft store. None of the companies that make those brands of paper are very environmentally friendly. You do some more research and find a company that uses recycled paper and pays to plant more trees. The environmentally friendly paper is more expensive, and you have to wait for it to be shipped to you online. You think about it for a little while, and decide the ethical thing to do is to buy the paper. You might have to charge a little more for your cards, but you feel great about using ethical materials.

You make cards and start selling them. You find out people love your cards! You make $500 in just a few weeks. Now what? You could spend all that money on yourself and buy a new TV. You could save it. You could use it to buy more paper and materials for your business, and start advertising. But remember, one of your goals starting out was to help other people. You have a

Business & Ethics

Organizations like Food From the 'Hood work to help the people in their communities and make money, combining their ambitions and their ethics.

decision to make, now that you have all this money. You do want your business to be successful, so you decide to use half of the $500 to advertise. You also want to go to college someday, so you save $150 in your bank account. You have $100 left, which you decide to donate to an animal rescue charity. You're practicing corporate responsibility!

Ethics and Goal-Setting

Food From the 'Hood

In 1992, people in Los Angeles were angry that white police officers had beaten a black man, Rodney King. The police officers weren't punished, and people got angry and rioted. In the end, hundreds of people were hurt or killed in the riot.

Lots of people were deeply moved by what happened. One group of high school students at Crenshaw High School in Los Angeles decided to do something to promote peace. They were upset about what was happening, and they wanted to help fix their community. They decided to turn some empty space into a garden and help feed hungry people. During their first few months, they figured out how to grow vegetables and donated all of the food they grew to a homeless shelter.

So far, the high schoolers were running a **nonprofit**. They used all the money they had to make donations, not make more money. But after a little while, the Crenshaw students brought their produce to a local farmers' market. They sold $150 of veggies in a half an hour. They were on to a business idea!

When they figured out they could make money with their garden, they didn't leave ethics behind. Pretty much everything they did to make money also was meant to help the community. They turned unused space into beautiful gardens, which made the neighborhood nicer. They continued to donate produce to people in need. They worked toward peace in the neighborhood.

Asija Chappel, a student who was part of the Food From the 'Hood business said, "Now that I'm a senior, I realize that the time I've spent in Food From the 'Hood is one of the best **investments** I have ever made. . . . Food From the 'Hood is an important resource for the students involved, the school, and the

Business & Ethics

community as a whole." Food From the 'Hood has a great ethical goal. The students behind it have worked hard to make money *and* help their community.

Ethics and Goal-Setting

THREE

Employee Ethics

It's hard enough making business decisions on your own. Throw some employees in there, and making ethical decisions can get even stickier!

Hiring Employees

As your business grows and makes more money, you might someday want to think about hiring employees. Employees will help your business grow even more, after a little investment.

In your imaginary greeting card business, for example, you start off just by yourself. You don't have enough money to pay for an employee. And you can handle all the work. After a few months, though, you start to get more work than you can handle.

Employees may act unethically for reasons that aren't clear at first. Perhaps an employee needs money to pay a bill, so she takes a few dollars from the cash register. Maybe an employee's workload has him so stressed that he cuts corners he wouldn't normally.

Business & Ethics

You don't want to turn people away when they hire you to make cards. And you don't want to give up going to craft fairs to sell your cards. Instead, you decide to hire an employee. You have a friend who is really good at drawing. You ask her if she wants to join your business. You explain you can pay her $2 a card, and she has to make at least ten cards a week. She says yes! Now you have an employee who can help your business grow.

Hiring an employee means your business is directly affecting more people. You need to treat your employees ethically to run a good business. Ask yourself if you're being fair to them and treating them with respect.

Going back to our example, your new employee is doing a great job at making cards. In fact, she's even better than you. You start to get jealous about how creative she is. Instead of telling her she's doing a good job, though, you tell her she's a bad artist and she needs to do better. She gets upset and threatens to quit.

You're not being very ethical in this situation. You let your jealousy get in the way of your business. And you're not being very nice to your friend! You hurt her feelings, and you also might lose an employee who is helping your business grow. After a little while, you realize you should change how you're acting because you're being unfair. You tell your employee that you really do think she's a great artist, and that you want her to stay at your company. You apologize for being unfair.

You also may have to deal with your employees doing unethical things. Say your new employee tells you she made twelve cards one week, instead of ten. You're thrilled! You don't bother to count them when she hands them to you—you just give her $24. The next week, she says she made thirteen cards and hands you a stack. This time you count them to make sure. There are

Employee Ethics　37

actually only ten in the stack. You ask her about the missing three, and she says she actually didn't make them.

You're not sure what the ethical thing to do is, so you think about it for a while. You don't think you should fire her, because she's a good artist and is helping your business. Her actions could also have been a lot worse, and she told you what was happening when you asked her. You decide to talk to her some more. You explain you're going to have her make the cards while you're watching. Then you'll know exactly how many cards she makes. Plus, you'll have fun hanging out, making cards together. And you'll learn how to be a better boss, and keep track of all the products you sell.

Whenever you're dealing with difficult employee situations, take a minute to think. Ask yourself what the right thing to do is. You can also talk to other people like your family or a teacher. You might actually already know what the right thing to do is, but you're hesitating because it's hard to do. For example, you know your employee is doing something wrong when she lies to you, but it can be hard to **confront** her about it. Part of being ethical is doing the right thing, even when it's hard.

You as an Employee

Lots of young people end up being employees at a company—maybe you're one of them. Being an employee of another company can be a great way to figure out how to run your own business. Perhaps someday you want to own your own car repair business. You've spent a lot of time fixing up old cars, but you don't know much about running a business. You can go work for someone else who has a car repair business to learn how it's done.

LIVING AN ETHICAL LIFE

Most people try to make ethical decisions—but it's not always clear if we're leading ethical lives or not. The Markkula Center for Applied Ethics lists a few questions to ask yourself every day, to see if you're being as ethical as you can be. You can ask them about yourself as a businessperson, or as a regular person:

1. Did I practice any **virtues** today? Good virtues include honesty, trustworthiness, compassion, and responsibility.
2. Did I do more good than harm today?
3. Did I treat people with **dignity** and respect today?
4. Was I fair and **just** today?
5. Was my community better today because I was in it?

If you can say yes to these questions every day, you're living an ethical life! If you say no once in a while, think about how you can change your actions. We all make mistakes sometimes, but we can always work to be more ethical people.

As an employee, you'll come across some situations where it's hard to decide what to do. You'll need to learn how to make ethical business decisions. At the car repair company, for example, you might work with another person who is older and more

Employee Ethics 39

Calling in sick when you're not isn't ethical behavior and can damage the trust between you and your employer. Calling in sick when you're too ill to work or might get others sick is completely ethical.

Business & Ethics

experienced than you. One day, you catch her putting some tools in her bag. You ask her what she's doing. She says her wrench at home is rusty, so she's taking a couple from the business for herself.

You ask yourself what you should do. Should you ignore what the other employee did and pretend you never saw her stealing? Should you tell your boss? You decide your boss should know. You don't feel great about telling on your coworker, but stealing is wrong. She might steal more things from your boss, who has worked really hard to buy all his tools and keep his business going. Her theft will cost him money, and it could even damage the business, so that it can't afford as many employees. Once you tell your boss, it will be up to him to decide what to do. In this case, you made an ethical decision.

A few weeks later, your friend invites you to go to the movies with him. You really, really want to go, but you have to work. You decide you want to see the movie so much that you're going to call in sick. You call and tell your boss you're not feeling well, and you go to the movie instead. As you're leaving the theater, you see your boss going into a hardware store. Even worse, he sees you! Now he knows you were lying.

In this situation, you made an unethical decision. You made your boss's life harder by skipping out on work when he needed you. You also made your own life harder, because now your boss will get mad at you. He also might not trust you anymore, and he probably won't let you have the same freedom at work you had before. The good news is that you'll remember what happened—and you'll make more ethical decisions in the future.

Ethical Employees

Food From the 'Hood has great business ethics, including when it comes to its employees. The business is run entirely by high school students called student managers. They do all the work, from planting the gardens, to advertising, to managing the money. The business is meant to help them.

One of the business's goals is to help get student employees into college after high school. In fact, 50 percent of the **profits** Food From the 'Hood makes go into a scholarship fund. (The other 50 percent is used to keep the business growing.) Each student employee ends up with between $2,000 and $3,000 to spend on college, depending on how much time and effort he or she has put in to the company. The money makes a lot of difference for students who may not otherwise be able to afford college. By 2007, the business had given out $200,000 in scholarships to almost eighty student managers.

Food From the 'Hood treats all employees with respect. The company gives employees something to do and a sense of accomplishment. Instead of hanging around with nothing to do or turning to violence, the young people who run Food From the 'Hood work hard and make a positive difference. Tammy Bird, a cofounder of Food From the 'Hood says, "It's a place for them to do their homework. It's a place to do college preparatory. It's a place to do their business and pick up entrepreneurial skills." Employees also can take advantage of tutoring, test preparation, and help with college applications.

Students also learn about ethics by being a part of Food From the 'Hood. Terie Smith, a former employee, said, "Food From the 'Hood is a business but it teaches much more. We learn how to take responsibility for our actions, how to set priorities, and

Business & Ethics

how to be leaders instead of followers." Employees like Terie have learned how to be their best and make the most ethical business decisions. The employees are treated ethically, and they also learn how to treat others ethically.

FOUR

Marketing Ethics

O nce you get involved in your own business, you'll have to figure out marketing. Marketing is how you **promote** your product. Marketing is the key to convincing other people to buy what you're selling.

You could start a business and then just sit there. You probably won't get too many customers. You need to tell people your business exists and what it's all about. The people who like what they hear will start to hire you or buy your products. But just like with other parts of business, you'll need to think about ethics when it comes to marketing.

With so many ways to draw customers to your company online and in print, why waste time with negative advertising? Sales, special offers, and honest advertising are a much better way to grow your business.

Business & Ethics

Advertising

You've seen advertisements all over the place—online, on TV, in magazines, on billboards, and on the sides of buses. All of those ads are telling you to buy something. Should you believe them?

That depends on if the company doing the advertising is ethical or not. An unethical company will make advertisements that are misleading. An unethical company might also attack other companies' products in their ads, to convince people their product is better. The *tactic* of attacking other businesses is called negative advertising.

You have some decisions to make when you're advertising your own business. First, you have to decide where you want to advertise. You can pass out flyers, post ads at school or at the public library, use Facebook, and send e-mails. You also have to decide how you want to advertise, and what you want to say with your ads.

Say your greeting card business is growing, but you think you could be making more money and selling to more people. It's time for advertising. You put up some posters around town, advertising exactly what you do. A few days later, you notice someone else has also put up ads for a greeting card business. Unfortunately, the ads attack your business and say bad things about it.

The ads make you really angry. You want to put up more flyers that attack the other business. Then you stop and think. You don't want to be like the other businessperson and post mean ads. You want to do the right thing. You put around some new ads that look really nice but don't say anything about the other business.

You made the ethical decision. People who see both ads also think you made the right decision. You have new customers come to you to buy cards. They tell you they saw your ads, and they

Marketing Ethics   47

decided to buy your cards because they didn't like how unfair the other business was. They appreciated that you were ethical and didn't attack back. Your ethical decision paid off!

Product Promises

Sometimes a business makes a false promise when marketing a product. For an example of unethical product promises, think of cigarette companies a few decades ago. Cigarette companies used to say cigarettes were healthy, and that cigarettes would not make people sick. Of course that's a lie, and the companies knew it was a lie. The companies' unethical behavior meant lots of people decided to keep smoking cigarettes. A lot of those people later got sick and even died.

Cigarette companies are a pretty extreme example of unethical promises. But even smaller businesses run by young people can fall into the trap of promising people the wrong things.

Maybe you're thinking of starting a tutoring business. You get pretty good grades in most subjects, except history, and you like teaching other people. Great! Tutoring sounds like the perfect job for you.

You start up your business, and you have to decide how you're going to market yourself. You tell everyone you know you're starting a tutoring business, and you set up a website. You also don't quite tell the truth. You tell people you can tutor in any subject, even history. Your website promises your students will get A's in the subjects you're helping them with. You figure if you can promise good grades, people will be more likely to hire you. And you're right—lots of people hire you to tutor them. You even have a few history students.

Things go great for a little while, but then the semester ends. A few of your harder-working students do get A's. Lots of them don't, though. The students you tutored in history do pretty poorly. They get mad, and they demand their money back.

You marketed yourself unethically. You misled people into thinking you were good at history. You also made promises you couldn't keep. The more ethical thing to do would have been to list the subjects you could tutor, and leave history off the list. You should also have avoided making any promises. Instead of promising A's, you could have told customers that if they worked hard and paid attention, they would likely start to see better grades. You're not promising anything, and you're encouraging your students to be part of the process. Luckily, you have enough

Marketing Ethics

customers who were happy with your tutoring, and you start making these more ethical decisions for the next semester.

Selling Ethically

Food From the 'Hood has successfully and ethically marketed their products. The business started out with a small garden, selling produce at a local farmers' market. After a customer at the market suggested they make their company bigger, the students at Crenshaw High School did some product and marketing research. They decided to expand into a salad dressing business.

The students successfully sold their idea to Sweet Adelaide, a **manufacturer** in anther town. Sweet Adelaide agreed to help them turn their idea for salad dressing into a real product. The first salad dressing they made was called Straight Out the Garden Creamy Italian Dressing. They added NoFat Honey Mustard two years later, and eventually Ranch Dressing.

After the students figured out how to make the dressings, they had to figure out how to sell them. They marketed their product to stores in the area and convinced many of them to put it on their shelves. They also started selling it on Amazon.com, where they had to market it to anyone who might come across it. After a few years of hard work, Food From the 'Hood sold salad dressing at two thousand stores and was making $250,000 a year! The company clearly knew how to market to the right people.

Food From the 'Hood wasn't done, though. The business got even bigger. In New York, the students started another company that sold applesauce. Some student employees also spread the word about the success of their **business model**. They thought struggling students all over the world could start companies like Food from the 'Hood. A few students traveled to London. They

visited a high school and gave the students there advice on how to start a company like Food From the 'Hood. In the United States, they inspired two groups in the Midwest and on the East Coast to start Food From the 'Hood companies.

The Crenshaw High School students learned as they went. They didn't know much about marketing a business when they started. But they worked hard, and they made the right decisions. The fact that they ran an ethical business helped them sell their idea to manufacturers, stores, and other schools. Ethical decisions lead to business success!

PRIORITIES

☑ Customer

☑ Customer

☐ Customer

FIVE

Ethics and Customers

One of your business goals should be to get as many customers as possible. But you shouldn't be willing to do just anything to get them. With that attitude, you could end up doing some pretty unethical things along the way. Treating your customers ethically will go a long way to making them happy. And happy customers equal loyal customers!

Treating Customers Ethically

The way you treat your customers is called customer service ethics. Think about it—when you go to a restaurant, get your hair cut, or buy something at the mall, you want the person serving you to be nice and friendly. You don't want the waiter to spit in your food, or the hairdresser to tell you you're ugly. Now flip it around. You don't want to treat your own customers unethically.

Treating customers ethically can be as simple as being nice to them. Customer service ethics also involve tougher situations. For example, as a small business owner, you have to be honest to your customers.

At your babysitting business, you try to always be honest with your customers. However, one time you almost slip up. The parents who hired you told you to put their two-year-old to bed at seven. They're coming home at nine. But you love to play with their kid, and he doesn't want to go to sleep at seven. You let him stay up, playing and watching TV, until right before nine. He's sleeping in bed by the time his parents walk in. The parents ask you if everything went OK, and if he went to sleep at seven.

You could say yes. Maybe they would never know the difference. If you told them you kept him up, they might not want to hire you again. But if you don't tell them, the next day might be hard for them. Their child will be sleepy and cranky, and the parents won't know why.

The ethical thing to do, though, is to tell them. Because you know honesty is the right thing to do, you tell the parents what happened. You explain that you really like spending time with their child, but you now understand what you did wasn't right. You offer them a discount and tell them it won't happen again. The parents are a little disappointed, but they appreciate that you told the truth. They even decide to hire you for the next weekend, although they tell you they're going to call you around seven to make sure their child is in bed.

Unethical Customers

Even if you're doing your job, and doing it ethically, you might run across an unethical customer. Unethical customers can be hard to deal with, but if you stay ethical, you'll do the right thing.

Let's go back to your greeting card business. You're doing well, and selling cards at lots of craft fairs. Some of your customers buy your cards whenever they see you. One in particular likes to buy at least two.

At one fair, this customer comes up to you and shows you a card he bought from you last week. He shows you where it's ripped on the inside, and asks if he could get another card. You agree, because you like to keep your customers happy, and he takes both cards with him. A week later, the same thing happens. You're starting to get suspicious. You look at all your cards before you sell them, and you don't remember any of them being ripped. You still want to keep the customer happy, so you let him take another card.

When the same thing happens for a third time, you know something is wrong. Your customer is lying to you to get free cards! You still want to be nice, but this customer isn't treating you fairly. When he tries to get another card this time, you refuse. He gets angry and tells you he's never going to buy cards from you again.

Sometimes doing the ethical thing ends up hurting you a little. In this case, you might have lost a customer. Your customers have the right to choose not to hire you or buy your product again if they're unhappy, but you know you did the ethical thing, and will learn what to do in the future.

Making the World a Better Place

Businesses can be great for you, for your community, and for the world. As long as we make ethical business choices, businesses can make the world a better place.

THE SIX PILLARS OF CHARACTER

Character is a big part of ethics. Character is basically who you are. Here are some good character qualities (and explanations of each) that lead to ethical behavior, according to the Josephson Institute Center for Youth Ethics:

- Trustworthiness: Be honest; don't deceive, cheat, or steal; be reliable—do what you say you'll do; have the courage to do the right thing; build a good **reputation**; be loyal—stand by your family, friends, and country
- Respect: Treat others with respect; follow the Golden Rule; be tolerant and accepting of differences; use good manners, not bad language; be considerate of the feelings of others; don't threaten, hit or hurt anyone; deal peacefully with anger, insults, and disagreements
- Responsibility: Do what you are supposed to do; plan ahead; **persevere**: keep on trying!; always do your best; use self-control; be **self-disciplined**; think before you act—consider the consequences; be accountable for your words, actions, and attitudes; set a good example for others
- Fairness: play by the rules; take turns and share; be open-minded—listen to others; don't take advantage of others; don't blame others carelessly; treat all people fairly
- Caring: Be kind; be compassionate and show you care; express **gratitude**; forgive others; help people in need

- Citizenship: do your share to make your school and community better; cooperate; get involved in community affairs; stay informed; vote; be a good neighbor; obey laws and rules; respect authority; protect the environment; volunteer

Food From the 'Hood is a perfect example of an ethical business that is making a positive difference. Asija Chappel, one of the former student managers of Food From the 'Hood says, "Those of us who are a part of Food From the 'Hood know that we belong to an organization that is truly unique. We have the chance to experience what most people don't until adulthood. We learn valuable skills, we form close relationships with the other members, and most importantly, we have fun."

Carlos Lopez, another student, adds, "It doesn't matter what you look like or where you live. If you can dream it, you can achieve it—and as you see, we are achieving it."

The business started by these two students, and many more, added a lot to their lives and their community. Food From the 'Hood provided fresh food for hungry people, trained employees for college, and successfully marketed their veggies and salad dressing to thousands of customers, all by choosing the ethical path.

Try to make your own business as ethical and positive as this one. You might make a few mistakes along the way, but before you know it, business ethics will be a natural part of your life.

Find Out More

Online

Bizinate
www.bizinate.com

Character and Ethics
www.42explore2.com/character.htm

The Mint
www.themint.org/kids/be-your-own-boss.html

These Kids Mean Busines$
www.thesekidsmeanbusiness.org/the_inside_story/index.php

In Books

Brown, Jeff. *The Kid's Guide to Business*. Newmarket, Ont.: TeachingKidsBusiness.com, 2003.

Sember, Brette McWhorter. *The Everything Kids' Money Book*. Avon, Mass.: F+W Media, 2008.

Weinstein, Bruce. *Is It Still Cheating If I Don't Get Caught?* New York: Roaring Brook Press, 2009.

Vocabulary

Bribing: giving someone money so they will treat you especially well.

Business model: a design for a successful company.

Cloning: making a genetically identical copy of a living thing.

Compassion: sympathy and understanding.

Confront: to deal with a difficult situation.

Corporate: relating to business.

Dignity: a sense of pride and respect.

Dilemmas: situations in which one must make a difficult choice.

Entrepreneurs: people who take risks to start businesses.

Ethnicity: the state of belonging to a social group that has a shared history or culture.

Genes: the tiny parts of living things that contain information passed on from parents to offspring.

Gratitude: thanks.

Investments: the time, money, or effort put into something to reach a goal.

Just: fair.

Low-income: not having a lot of money.

Manufacturer: a person or company that physically makes products, usually in a factory.

Nonprofit: an organization that uses the money it makes to further a social cause.

Persevere: to keep going.

Policies: courses of action undertaken by a government.

Profits: the money a business makes, after taking into account the money spent to start the business.

Promote: to advertise or encourage.

Qualities: the distinguishing properties of someone's personality.

Reputation: the general way other people see you.

Resources: a supply of money, time, and materials used to run a business.

Self-disciplined: able to control oneself

Sociologist: a person who studies how humans organize themselves into societies.

Swindled: lied to someone to get money from them.

Tactic: an action planned to have a specific effect; one part of a larger strategy.

Values: beliefs; things people think are important.

Virtues: qualities considered good in a person.

Index

About the Author and Consultant

James Fischer received his master's in education from the State University of New York, and went on to teach life skills to middle school students with learning disabilities.

Brigitte Madrian is the Aetna Professor of Public Policy and Corporate Management at the Harvard Kennedy School. Before coming to Harvard in 2006, she was on the faculty at the University of Pennsylvania Wharton School (2003–2006), the University of Chicago Graduate School of Business (1995–2003) and the Harvard University Economics Department (1993–1995). She is also a research associate and co-director of the Household Finance working group at the National Bureau of Economic Research. Dr. Madrian received her PhD in economics from the Massachusetts Institute of Technology and studied economics as an undergraduate at Brigham Young University. She is the recipient of the National Academy of Social Insurance Dissertation Prize (first place, 1994) and a two-time recipient of the TIAA-CREF Paul A. Samuelson Award for Scholarly Research on Lifelong Financial Security (2002 and 2011).

Picture Credits